For my mother

Printed in Great Britain
First US edition

1 2 3 4 5 6 7 8 9 10

Library of Congress Cataloging in Publication Data

Ormerod, Jan.
   101 things to do with a baby.

   Summary: A six-year-old girl tells 101 things she can do with her baby brother.
   [1. Babies – Fiction. 2. Brothers and sisters – Fiction]
I. Title. II. Title: One hundred one things to do with a baby.
III. Title: One hundred and one things to do with a baby.
PZ7.0634Aad 1984   [E]   84-4401
ISBN 0-688-03801-8
ISBN 0-688-03802-6

101 Things to do with a Baby

JAN ORMEROD

Lothrop, Lee &
Shepard Books,
New York

1 say good morning

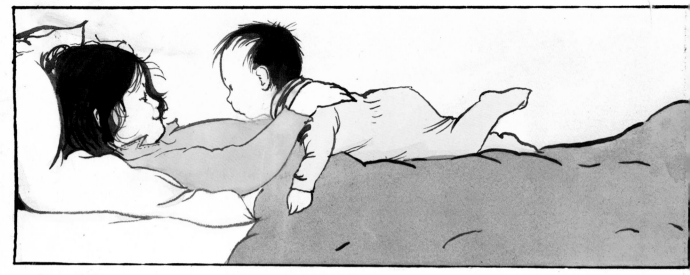

2 play with baby before breakfast

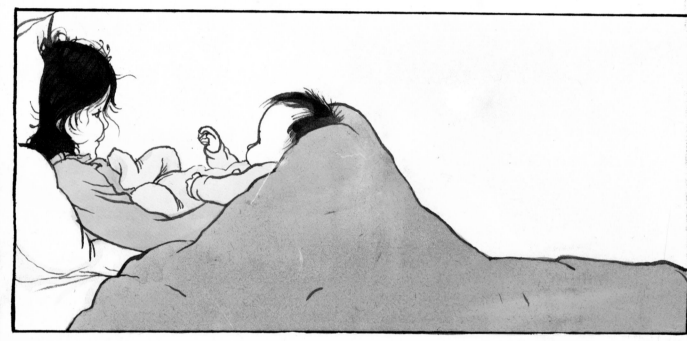

3 put him in his special chair

4 give him cereal

5 and let him share your egg

6 better clean him up

7 let's do the washing

8 put it in the machine

9 add the soap powder

10 watch it whizz around

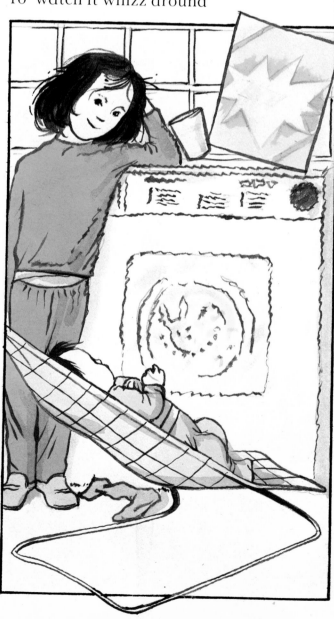

11 spy him in his bouncing chair

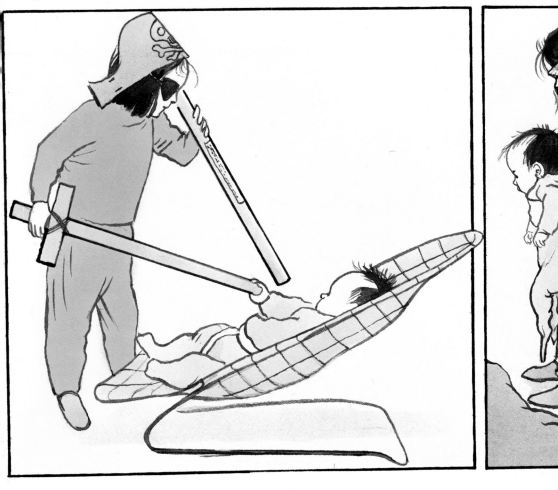

12 put him on the floor

13 for a chat

14 exercise his legs

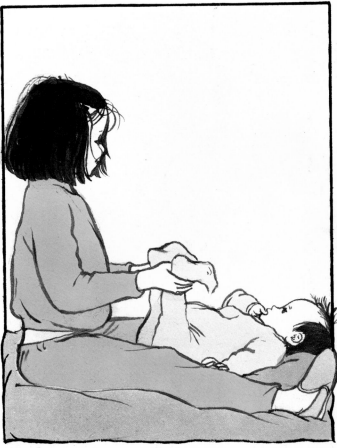

15 now do sit ups

16 or stand ups

17 or push ups

18 see how we can stretch

19 twist left

20 twist right

21 and roll over

22 now knees up all together

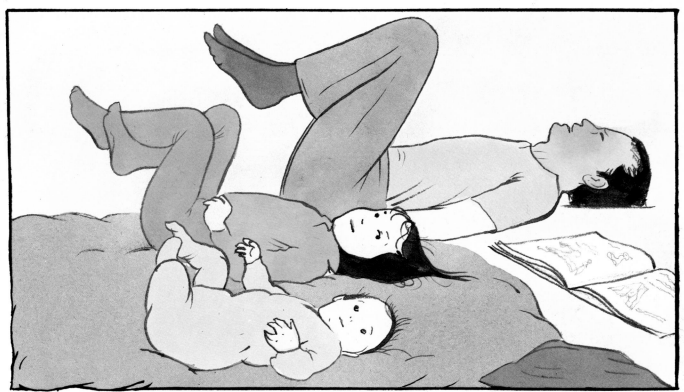

23 and then relax

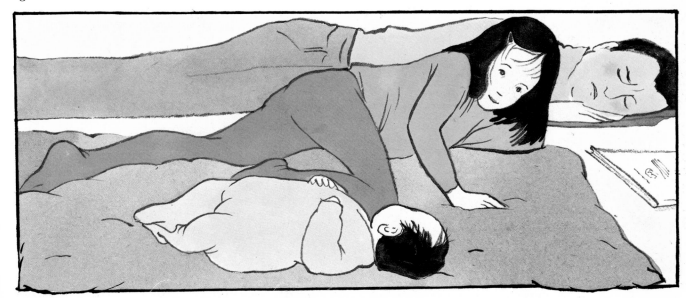

24 put on rubber boots   25 and a plastic apron   26 get the mop

27 the baby's bath   28 and a nice soft towel

29 not too hot

30 put in the bubbles

31 froth them up

32 put in the baby

33 and dodge the splashes

37 kiss him better

38 whisper a secret

39 tickle his tummy

40 and give him some toys

watch out for . . .

41 hair pulling

42 nose grabbing

43 dribbling

44 and drooling

45 watch out for shoe sucking

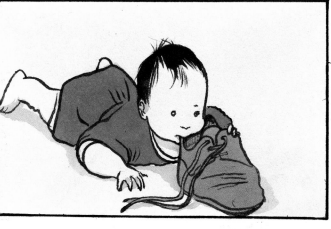

46 letter eating

47 ankle biting

48 head banging

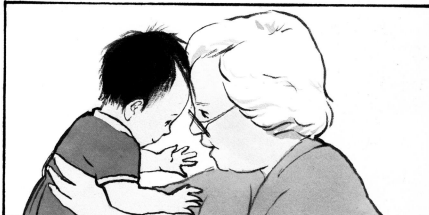

49 and watch out for Granny's glasses

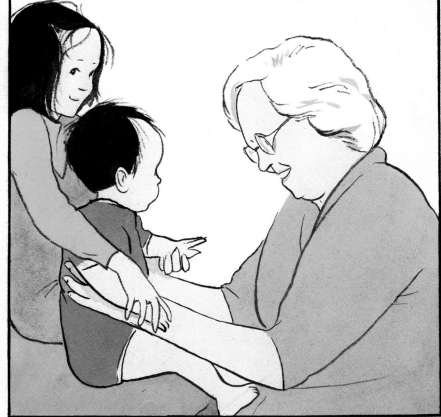

50 hang out the washing

51 rock baby to sleep

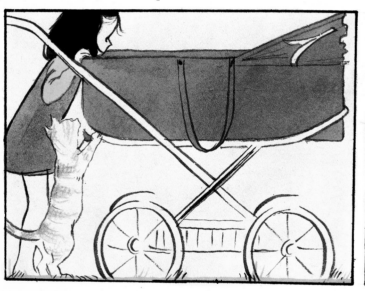

52 shoo away the cat

53 make a daisy chain

54 and look out for rain

55 bring the washing in again

56 hide

57 play peep

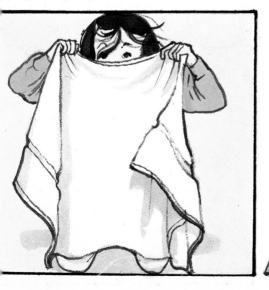

58 say boo

59 try on Mother's hat

60 or Father's shoes

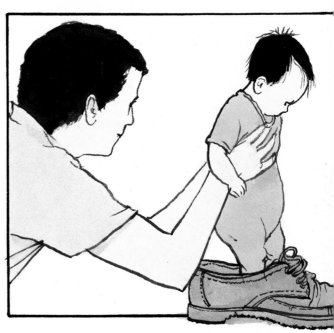

61 put him in his crib for a quiet tim

62 dress up in his wrap

63 play with his teddy

64 build with his blocks

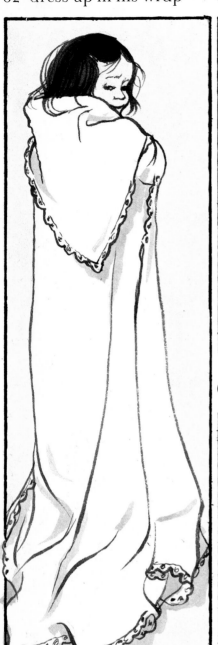

65 or borrow his basket

until he wakes up again

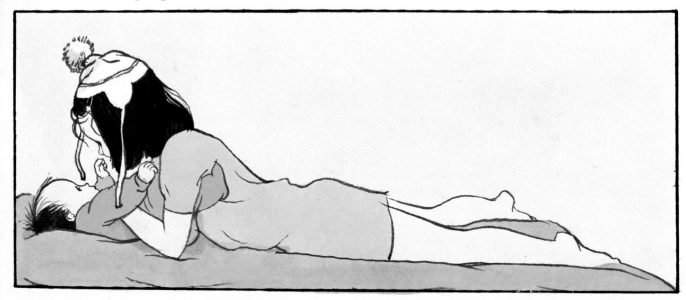

66 touch his nose

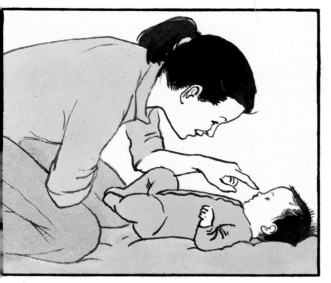

67 walk up from his toes

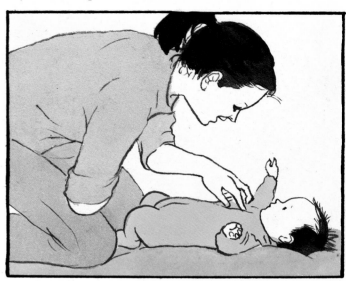

68 kiss his ear or

69 blow on his tummy

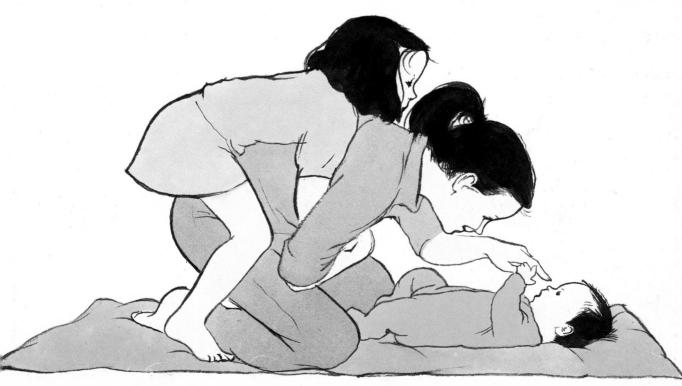

72   take him in the car

73   or take him on a picnic

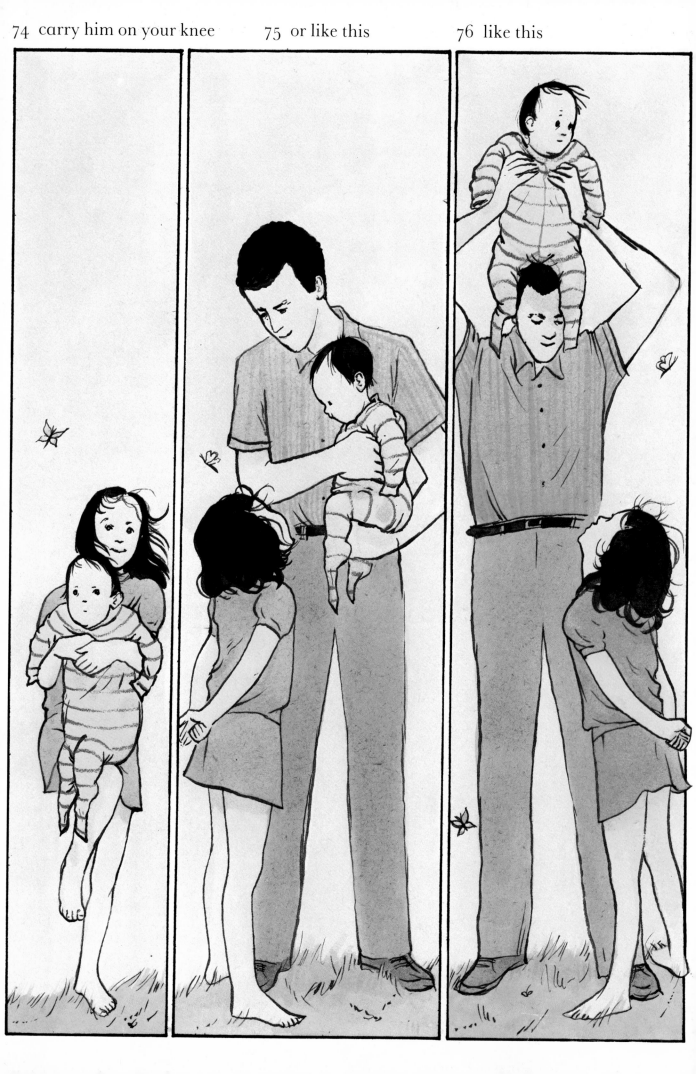

80 collect rocks

81 leaves

82 bugs

83 and flowers for him

but not to eat

84 let him meet big dogs

85 babies

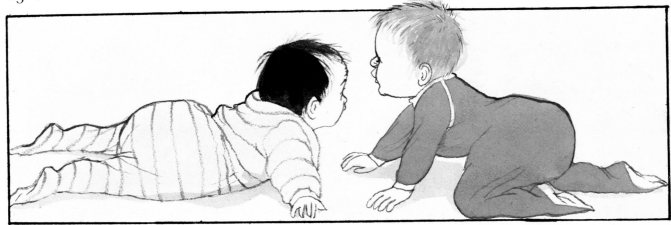

86 snails

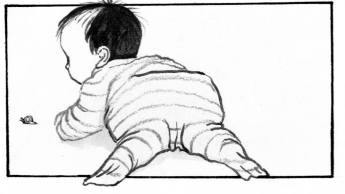

87 and fish

88 roll him up in a rug

89 make him a baby box

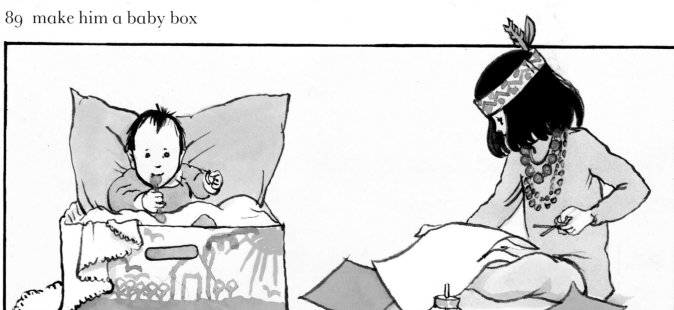

90 take him into your tent with you

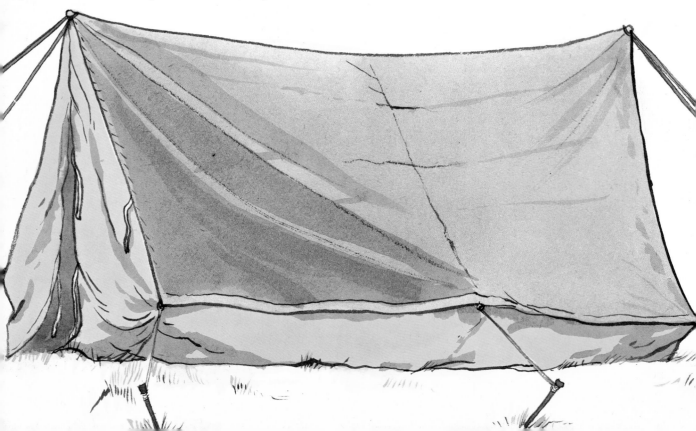

try him in his bouncing chair

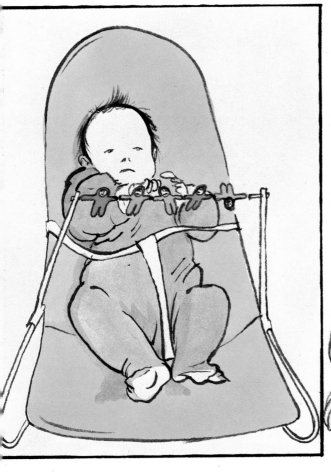

try him with a book

try him with some rattling toys

94 or let him sit with you

95 watch television together

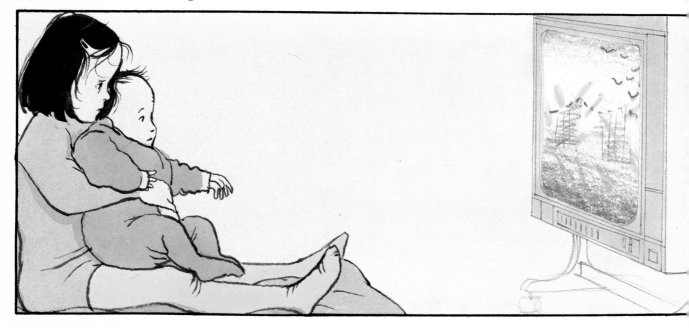

until he's bored

96 give him a book to read

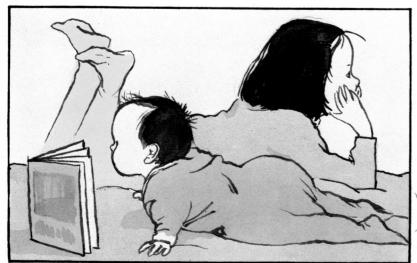

97 but not to chew or tear

98 shout at him

99 and make him cry

100 give him a cuddle

101 and a kiss good night